Foreword

The creation of a book describing the birds of Lee Abbey has been a long time in the making. For a number of years *Chris Baillie* has surveyed birds from the estate on a monthly basis. This arrangement was borne out of Lee Abbey's partnership with the Christian conservation charity *A Rocha*, who share Lee Abbey's aim of promoting the value and importance of conservation and environmental sustainability. Without Chris' faithful groundwork the data behind this book would not exist. I owe him a special debt of gratitude for the scientific and thorough way in which species have been recorded here.

From Spring 2012 I've had the privilege of taking some of Lee Abbey's guests on 'bird listening' walks around the estate. In those few weeks in spring the woodlands come alive with birdsong, and introducing the sounds of the songsters to keen observers has been a thrilling experience. However, these walks are limited to the few weeks of the year when birds are in their best voice, and I've been challenged to produce something that would be an available resource all year round. As well as developing an audio-visual presentation, my aim was to produce something that a guest or visitor to Lee Abbey could take away with them from their time here.

Producing a book about the birds that occur at Lee Abbey Devon has thrown up a few questions; most notably, which birds to realistically include and which to omit. To keep the book to a manageable extent, I have included species that are most common at Lee Abbey, together with some 'speciality' species that can reasonably be expected to be found at some time of the year or other. There are many other birds on the data list that have been recorded over the years, but they mainly constitute irregular or occasional sightings *(see appendix at the back of the book)*.

I have been helped enormously by *Andrew Painting*, who took on the task of the main species writing with relish. I've only been severe with my editing of his copy in places because space does not permit me to include everything he'd written. *Danny Russell* came along at just the right time, offering to provide some line drawings, which make the book a more attractive offering. I'm grateful to him for his eye for detail and keenness to help.

Special thanks go also to *Rachel Oates*, Lee Abbey's Environmental Co-ordinator, for her help in getting this project off the ground. Thanks also go to *Sophie Davis* for being willing to proofread the manuscript at short notice. Special mention goes to *Pixie Rowe* for her support and encouragement in bringing the project to completion. Her experience gained in the production of the *Lee Abbey Tea Cottage Cookbook* has been a great help in realising the potential of this particular volume. And finally, I am indebted to the late *Ursula Kay*, who was an inspiration for all things nature-related in her time at Lee Abbey and whose book *He Gave us Eyes to See Them* lives on to this day some thirty years hence. The centre spread contains three of her delightful studies from 1980 that never made it to print.

Andrew Mann, Lee Abbey, July 2014.

Introduction by Chris Baillie
Birds through the seasons at Lee Abbey

With woodland, fields, cliffs, sea and adjacent moorland – Lee Abbey Devon offers an opportunity to enjoy a wide variety of birds, with over 70 species occurring during a year. Familiar garden birds are here but you may also see the fastest bird on the planet (the Peregrine Falcon), breeding Redstarts or, occasionally, sightings of Gannets out to sea. A few are obvious, others will be found with patience. Largely it will depend upon the time of year and where you look.

Winter (November-February)
The woods are very quiet (although Robins sing most of the year), but with the leaves fallen, it can be a good time to see species such as Treecreeper, Siskin, Marsh Tit, and Nuthatch. Blackcaps mostly move to the Mediterranean and beyond, but a small number overwinter here and one or two may sometimes be seen in the bushy areas of the woods. Herring Gulls return to the cliffs below Jenny's, followed later by Great Black-backed Gulls (neither species having been totally absent). Blue tits, Great tits, Coal tits, Goldfinches, Chaffinches, Robins, Dunnocks, Blackbirds and the occasional Great Spotted Woodpecker frequent the bird feeders outside the Orangery and at the Beacon. In snowy weather mixed flocks of Meadow Pipits, Redwings, Fieldfares and Starlings are driven down from higher ground to forage on Lee Abbey's sheltered fields.

Early Spring (March-April)
By early March Fulmars begin to claim cliff ledge nesting sites. Superficially resembling gulls but actually related to albatrosses, they were almost unknown in this area until the 1940s. Guillemots begin to visit cliff ledges to the west just beyond Woody Bay, joined by a smaller number of Razorbills around the end of March. Though distant, they can be seen arriving and leaving and on the water – Crock Point gives the best vantage point. Activity is highest in the early morning when you may see their exaggerated slow wing-beat display flights. Peregrines and Ravens are also early to their cliff nest sites, whilst the Rookery (you can't miss it!) becomes active and noisy. The woodland Sparrowhawk needs an early start on nesting too in order to have its young at the right stage to benefit later from a good supply of fledging song birds. Chiffchaff may first be noticed in hedges and bushes feeding up before flying across the Channel en route north from Africa. Soon those moving into the woods to breed will be staking out their territories with the repetitive song from which they get their name. Watch the fields for passing Wheatear.

Late Spring (April-May)

The dawn chorus is worth the effort as Garden Warbler, Willow Warbler and Whitethroat may be added to the other voices as the woodland breeding season gets underway. Spotted and Pied Flycatchers may be found and Blackcaps and House Martins can't be missed. Gannets (presumably from the Grassholm colony off Wales) are now regular off-shore and spectacular when plunge-diving for fish.

Summer (June-August)

Young birds hatch, fledge and fly. There is less song in the woods, but more birds – though some begin to disperse soon after the short period of depending on parents. Guillemots and Razorbills depart their cliff nest-sites during July and family parties can be seen out at sea.

Autumn (September-October)

By the end of August many of the migrant songbirds have moved out or are quiet. The noisy family parties of tits have mostly dispersed. From now through September it is sometimes possible to get a hint of migration. An early morning visit to the wooded cliff tops may produce a few willow warblers arrived overnight, whilst occasional small flocks of swallows may be seen arriving across the channel. By mid-October the woods are quiet, but Robins sing to stake out territories as the residents are joined by overwintering birds. Tawny Owls call nightly. A few House Martins may still be around if there have been late broods in their mud nests glued under the eaves of the main building. The first groups of Redwing and then Fieldfares arrive – probably moving through, though later flocks may become short-term residents. Gulls (so obvious most of the year) move off for a few weeks, and few sea birds are evident.

Key to abundance chart used in this book

The seasonal abundance chart uses a scale of 0-6 to indicate how likely a sighting (either visual or by song or call) of a species is in each month of the year at Lee Abbey. It is specific to the locality rather than to a wider region or national.

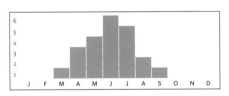

The scale is: 0 = unknown; 1 = rare; 2 = must be definitely sought; 3 = needs a bit of searching; 4 = seen most days; 5 = regularly seen; 6 = impossible to miss.

Index

Fulmar

A relation of the albatross, Fulmars breed along the cliffs of North Devon. They can resemble our resident Herring Gulls, having similar grey wings and white bodies. Look out for their short, curved bills and smaller bodies. In flight you can see their proportionally longer and straighter wings and fast, shallow wing beats. The best place to see Fulmars is the cliffs between Lee Abbey and the Valley of Rocks. In the breeding season, you can hear their manic, staccato cackle and watch them rear their young over the inaccessible cliff faces. The name 'Fulmar' comes from the Norse for 'foul gull' - a name relating to their habit of coughing up a sticky, oily liquid onto would-be predators.

Gannet

Easily recognised by their large, white bodies, creamy yellow heads and ink-dipped black wingtips, Gannets breed off of the Pembrokeshire coast and fly up the Bristol Channel to feed. Sometimes coming in quite close to shore, look out for the adult Gannet's yellow head and bright blue eyes. Younger birds can be harder to identify, being various shades of grey and brown, but with good views their large size, huge wingspan and 'paddling' flight makes them easy enough to pick out.

Gannets can be seen all year, but they are particularly noticeable between May and August. Look out for their famous 'plunge-diving' fishing technique; Gannets dive headfirst into the water at speeds of up to 6omph in pursuit of prey.

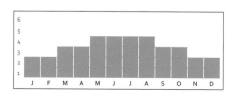

Oystercatcher

The piebald piper of the shoreline, the Oystercatcher is Lee Abbey's most common wader. Fond of not just oysters but all crustaceans, you can find them in small groups probing the shoreline with their bright red bills. These gregarious birds have a high-pitched, piping alarm call, which is generally delivered in a tone that can only be described as righteous indignation. 'How dare they go for a walk along the beach?' It says. 'I was feeding there.' Oystercatchers occur year round, but their numbers seem to peak around August to October, when resident birds are joined by new fledglings and migrants.

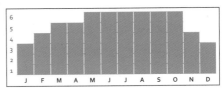

Cormorant

Ancient and ungainly-looking birds, Cormorants tend to be seen in the sheltered bays diving for fish or drying their wings on the rocks at the base of the cliffs. They also regularly fly past, head and neck extended, looking rather like a motley ocean-going goose. Cormorants are generally all-black with white/yellow bills but their plumage can be remarkably variable.

Herring Gull

Herring Gulls are the 'standard format' gull. With a stern expression, beady yellow eye and a tendency to steal people's ice creams, they can seem somewhat imposing. Herring Gulls are extremely intelligent and adaptable, particularly when it comes to food. Along with ice cream, they will scavenge everything from fish to worms to rubbish. Their calls are the most familiar of seaside sounds – think 'Desert Island Discs'.

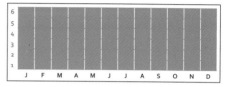

Great Black-backed Gull

Great Black-backed Gulls are huge, hulking giants, much larger than 'standard' Herring Gulls. Reasonably scarce, look out for their black backs and pink feet. These are the pirates around our waters, stealing food off of other gulls and anything else that happens to pass.

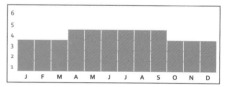

Lesser Black-backed Gull

The closely related, more common Lesser Black-backed Gulls are Herring Gull-sized, with a slate grey back and bright yellow feet.

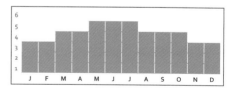

Guillemot

Guillemots are the more common of the two auk species which frequent the waters around Lee Abbey. They are dark-chocolate black above, white below, and have an irritating habit of diving underwater when you get your binoculars on to them. They nest in colonies on cliff faces.

Razorbill

Razorbills are a darker black than guillemots and slightly smaller, having a much heavier bill with traces of white about it. Like our other seabirds, razorbills are found during the breeding season, going further out of the channel during the winter.

Both auks are most often seen between April and August. Take the coast path between the Valley of Rocks and Lynton and keep an eye on the sea close in to the coast. You occasionally find small, mixed flocks of up to thirty birds on the water or flying above it with fast wingbeats.

View towards Castle Rock and the Lee Abbey Estate from the Coast Path in the Valley of Rocks. Look out to sea in the summer months for views of auks

Buzzard

Lee Abbey, with its mixture of woodland, open farmland and moorland, is perfect habitat for Buzzards. They are obvious in fine weather, when they soar on thermals above the grounds in big circles. While the Buzzard's plumage is notoriously variable, being various shades from white to dark brown to black, they can be easily told by their stubby 5-ft wingspan, wedge-shaped tail and mewing, 'cat-like' cry. Buzzards do exceptionally well in North Devon, breeding in quiet stretches of woodland and hunting and scavenging in the surrounding countryside. Watch out for 'mobbing' by crows, as a group will attack and chase off the larger Buzzard, apparently just for the fun of it.

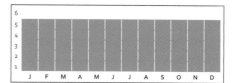

Sparrowhawk

Sparrowhawks are Kestrel-sized, with broad wings, a strikingly long tail and a fierce, wild expression. With a slate-grey back and striped front, Sparrowhawks can resemble any number of other birds of prey, particularly when they decide to soar on thermals. Look out for their broad wings and small size and long tail. Like most birds of prey the males are the smaller birds, and they can be up to a third smaller than the females. Males have a beautiful stripy orange front, and a bluer tinge to their grey backs. Sparrowhawks are mainly birds of woodland, farmland and gardens. They hunt small birds, flying low between trees in short bursts in a way that our other resident birds of prey could never do.

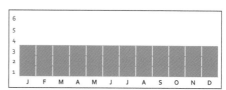

Kestrel

One of our most beautiful birds, the Kestrel is a small, rusty-red falcon. Males are smaller and smarter than the larger, spottier females, with a light grey head and small black moustaches. Kestrels are well known for their ability to hover in mid-air while hunting, as they search below them for everything from

mice and voles to insects. They can usually be found over the scrubby ground by the crosses and the surrounding fields as well as over the cliffs. Like all birds of prey, they are far more active when the weather is good, so wait for a nice day before venturing out to find them.

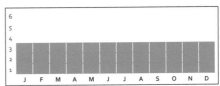

Peregrine Falcon

Peregrines are some of Lee Abbey's most spectacular residents. They are the quintessential falcon, with a charcoal grey head, steely back, a closely barred body and a vicious yellow beak and legs. These large falcons scythe through the air on stocky, pointed wings before diving on their prey at speeds exceeding 200mph. They can be seen all year scouring the cliffs for pigeons or flying high over the

buildings. The best time to see them is during the breeding season, when they are known to regularly breed on the cliffs at Woody Bay and the Valley of Rocks, and have probably bred on the Lee Abbey estate in the past.

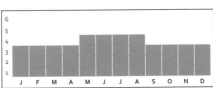

Pheasant

A rather abundant game bird, the Pheasant is commonly farmed in the area for shooting. Males are a mottled chestnut-red with ornate green and red heads and long, plumed tails. Females are smaller and drabber, though are still the size of a large chicken. Their call is a slightly disconcerting squawk, as though someone has trodden on their foot, and is generally accompanied by a lot of flustered wings as they loudly fly for cover after being startled. Pheasants can be seen readily in the fields, especially by the verges of the woodland where they roost. They are naturally at their most obvious between the breeding season and the shooting season.

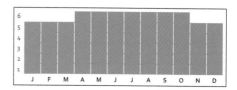

Moorhen

Told from Coots by their red, not white, head, Moorhens are actually a different family of bird altogether, being rails, not ducks. They are small, dumpy black birds with long yellow legs and spindly feet. Moorhens are seen anywhere that there is freshwater and long grass, and can be incredibly gregarious. Their call is a harsh, single cry, sounding not unlike the murder victim in an Agatha Christie novel.

Woodpigeon

By far the most common of the pigeons and doves of the area is the Woodpigeon. It is the largest of our pigeons, looking stout and stocky with a white, purple and green 'collar' around its neck. Listen out for its cooing. When startled, Woodpigeons fly off with an enormous clatter and fluster. In the breeding season, males will make display flights; flapping up high into the air and then gliding back down again.

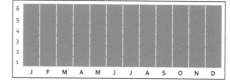

Tawny Owl

The woodlands around Lee Abbey play host to a healthy population of Tawny Owls. These are not the pale, screechy white spectres of night (those are either Barn Owls, or possibly ghosts); Tawny Owls are big, bulky brown owls with a large 'face' and eyes, of the type found in Winnie the Pooh. Responsible for the famous 'twit twoo' are actually two Tawny Owls; one first calling 'twit' and the other responding 'twoo'. In early winter it is possible to hear several Tawny Owls hooting all together.

Actually seeing the owls is of course much harder than hearing them, given as they are to nocturnal behaviour and being unsportingly well camouflaged. You are most likely to glimpse one at night, in the headlights of a car, either sitting low in a tree or occasionally on a fencepost.

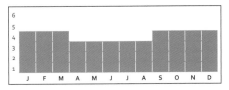

House Martin

Year after year House Martins nest around the guttering of the main building. First visible in late April, they are perhaps the most obvious summer visitors, as up to a hundred make up the colony. Dark blue/black above, white below, with a stubby forked tail and short stubby wings. It is best told from our other hirundine, the Swallow, by its white rump. The House Martins are a real highlight of the summer, with up to two hundred flying around the buildings. They regularly drop to the floor to bathe in dust, pick up nesting materials and even simply enjoy the warmth of the concrete. They leave our shores by early October.

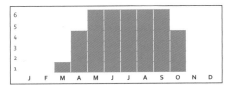

Rook

Rooks breed in colonies and are gregarious, noisy crows. The yew trees on the north side of the house host a colony which breeds in the spring and roosts in the winter. Similar in plumage to Carrion Crows with dark blue-black bodies and a bulky appearance, they are told apart by a white base to the bill, which gives the Rook its distinctive-looking face.

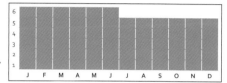

Jackdaw

Jackdaws are diminutive fellows, with beautiful pale blue eyes and smart, grey heads. These are much smaller than the Rooks, with which they can often be found. In direct sunlight you find that these birds are not black, but in fact a glossy, dark blue, occasionally even iridescent. Their call is more chatty than the harsh cawing of the Rook.

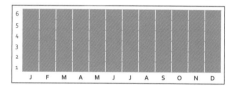

Carrion Crow

Away from the Rookery and wheeling overhead are the Carrion Crows: big, bulky and the standard-format crow. These birds tend not to flock in the same way as rooks and jackdaws but can often be found in small family groups. Look out for the all-black beak and their haughty demeanour.

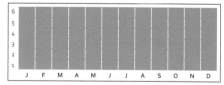

Jay

Jays are most usually seen flying away from you as a streak of pink and blue, yelling a hoarse, slightly unnerving scream as it does so. It is more likely to be found in woodland areas.

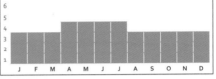

Magpie

The Magpie's bad press about killing songbirds is at best highly exaggerated and at worst completely erroneous. It is a common bird and is found in most habitats. Magpies are easy to identify with their pied plumage, long tail and grating cackling call.

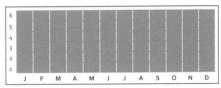

Raven

Ravens are regular in the Valley of Rocks and often make incursions into Lee Abbey airspace. Ravens can be tricky to separate from Carrion Crows; especially the big, well-fed Carrion Crows of North Devon. Ravens are noticeably bigger, but to be sure of their identification you'll need to look for the diamond-shaped tail and proportionally larger beak and head and longer, more pointed wings. Finally, listen out for their deep, booming croak – once you've heard it, it's unmistakable.

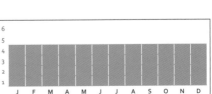

Green Woodpecker

The Green Woodpecker is, by all estimations, a slightly alarming-looking bird. A woodpecker, yes, but one that spends most of its time on the floor, foraging for ants and other insects. It is a vibrant green, with a black and red head, about the size of a woodpigeon. It is most often seen in flight; an awkward, loping pattern, which gives it the air of an enormous, gawky butterfly. Green Woodpeckers are most often seen in lightly wooded areas, with plenty of open ground for their foraging.

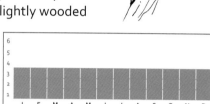

Great Spotted Woodpecker

The classic British woodpecker: black with white panels; the males have a red patch on the head. Once only found in woodland, Great Spotted Woodpeckers have seen a great increase in their population size since the birth of widespread feeding of birds in gardens. Their behaviour has also been reported to have changed - they are now much tamer than they were half a century ago and are regularly seen on bird tables around the country. The best place to see them at Lee Abbey, however, remains the densely wooded valleys.

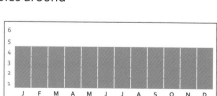

Skylark

The Skylark is well known for its beautiful song, but is rather underwhelming to look at. Larger and fatter than a Robin, Skylarks are a mottled brown and white with flecks of black and the white bands on the edge of its tail. Male Skylarks, aptly named, launch themselves into the sky, reeling off their song and parachuting back down to the ground in an almost disgracefully outlandish display. Because this song is seasonal Skylarks are often overlooked in winter.

Meadow Pipit

Meadow Pipits are stripy and brown, with long pink legs and relatively long tails. They are very common and frequent the pastures of Lee Abbey. Meadow Pipits often fly up

from the undergrowth when disturbed, revealing their white outer tail feathers, and in the breeding season they have a 'parachute' display flight. The Meadow Pipit's call is a high-pitched piping, usually at least half a dozen times in quick succession.

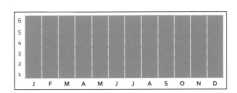

Rock Pipit

Rock Pipits are duller and usually darker in plumage than the Meadow Pipit and have a much more pronounced supercilium (eyebrow). They can be found on the beach. The Rock Pipit's call is a very high-pitched squeak, usually called three times in succession.

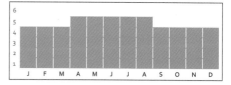

Pied Wagtail

Another well named bird: it is indeed black and white and it does indeed wag its tail. Found regularly in fields and car parks around Britain, and Lee Abbey is no exception. The Pied Wagtail is Robin sized, but with a tail nearly as long as the rest of its body. They are closely related to pipits, and share their fondness for insects. Pied Wagtails are particularly noticeable around the grounds and buildings of Lee Abbey. They have a tendency to bicker and fight along the rooftops and normally announce themselves with a shrill, nasal 'chizzit!'

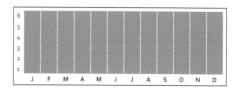

Look for Rock Pipits around the large rocks on Lee Abbey's beach, and watch where the stream runs into the sea for Grey Wagtails

Grey Wagtail

Reasonably well named. It's pretty yellow, but not as yellow as the Yellow Wagtail, which has unfortunately ceased to visit this part of the country. Grey above, black and yellow below, with the longest, waggiest tail of all the wagtails, the sure-fire way to tell it from Yellow Wagtails is the slate-grey face. Grey Wagtails love the fast-moving streams and rivers of the area. They also turn up regularly enough on the beach, perusing the rocks and weeds for insects. In winter they can be found further afield.

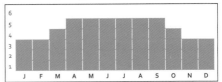

Wren

More mouse than bird, the wren, beloved of Christmas cards, is a solitary, skulking bird with a stubby, starched tail. All brown, darker above, with a small creamy supercilium (eyebrow), the tiny Wren is remarkably vocal. It sings all year round, a long piece of about four bars ending in a tremolo-trill. Once it is heard it is never forgotten. Look out for Wrens in woodland, woodpiles, and anything else with small holes to hide in and lots of insects to feast on.

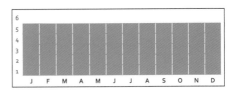

A family of Pied Flycatchers seen near the dam.

A male Chaffinch with very white wings has been around the Car Park area for over a year.

Buzzards wheeling overhead as the Hayfield is cut, — pouncing every so often on the easy prey of voles and mice disturbed by the mower.

Dipper

Small, fat and definitely not waterproof, Dippers live on the banks of the fast flowing streams that are a feature of North Devon, where they often bob up and down on a rock or plunge headfirst into raging torrents in search of insects. Thrush sized, Dippers have a glossy brown head and back, chestnut underparts and a gorgeous white front. Their calls are a high pitched 'zrik!', which can be heard amazingly clearly over the sound of raging rapids. They are incredibly strong swimmers; often navigating watercourses beyond the abilities of most humans. The stream by the Tea Cottage is a favoured location.

Dunnock

Formerly known as Hedge Sparrows, Dunnocks are really only very spuriously related to 'real' Sparrows, being part of an obscure family of birds known as accentors. They are superficially sparrow-esque, in that they are similar-sized, brown and stripy with pinkish-brown legs. Unlike sparrows, these are songbirds, having a sweet, if repetitive, song. Look out for their fine, insect-eating bill, grey face and skulky demeanour. Dunnocks like feeding on the floor and singing from the top of hedges. They are also pretty unsocial birds, never being seen in groups like real sparrows. You can see them year-round among the leaf litter of the woods and gardens.

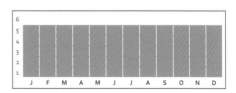

Robin

Another Christmas card favourite, with its unmistakable red breast, light brown back and white underparts. Robins are rather aggressive and exceptionally territorial (one of the leading causes of death among Robins is, in fact, other Robins). They are ubiquitous around the Abbey, but most often seen in lightly wooded areas and gardens. Like Blackbirds, Robins sing nearly all year round, from morning until dusk. Robins have a very complex song – a call and response act that involves much invention and practice. The Robin with the most complicated song is generally the one who gets to breed.

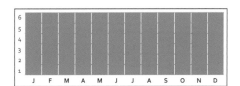

Redstart

Redstarts are migrants, closely related to Robins. Males have a glorious black front, slate-grey back and red underparts. Females are a little more tricky to identify, but look out for their uniform olive-brown back, warm and chestnut-red front. In flight their red tails, with a small black rectangle in the centre, are a good way of identifying them. Redstarts are reasonably rare in Britain; their breeding areas being confined to Wales and the West Country. They need a mixture of open pasture and pristine deciduous woodland, which Lee Abbey has in abundance. Check out fence posts on the edges of woodlands – these are often favourite perches as they inspect the ground for insects.

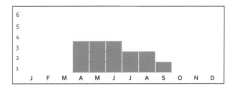

Stonechat

A walk through the Valley of Rocks would not be complete without spotting one or two of these charming birds. Related to Robins and Redstarts, Stonechats are slightly smaller. Males have a chocolately-black head, chestnut-red front and large white 'comma' around the neck. Again, females are more nondescript, as are the juveniles. Stonechats are by no means scarce or shy, but they do need a specific habitat of rough grazing land and moorland. Stonechats are prolific breeders, raising several broods each year. The Stonechat derives its name from its call: a repetitive, uninspiring 'chat', like two stones being knocked together. They also sing a high-pitched, scratchy song.

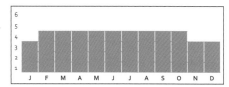

Wheatear

A summer migrant, Robin-sized Wheatears are named after their white rump. This is a very good way of identifying them - the white rump is apparent in males, females and juveniles alike, and is very noticeable when birds are in flight. As usual, males have the most interesting plumage, with a glorious slate-grey back, black face with a very obvious white 'eyebrow'. Females *(pictured)* and immature birds are drabber and in general appear to be a 'washed out' version of the males. Wheatears are again best seen in the Valley of Rocks but only during 'passage' periods (early April to early May, and September to October), when birds are migrating through the area from further north to their North African wintering grounds, they can turn up in pretty much any open ground.

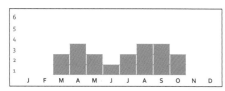

Blackbird

The most obvious of the thrushes, Blackbirds are common, tame and have a beautiful voice. Males are, quintessentially, black birds - the only colour being their bright orange bill, delicate and prominent. Females are a uniform, chocolate brown with an occasional light brown smudge on their chins. Juveniles, as is so often the case, resemble the females. Blackbirds are early singers, starting as early as January and singing from before sunrise. Theirs is a fruity, almost syrupy song; as complex as a Robin's but somewhat lower pitched and more flutey. Blackbirds also call an alarmed 'chuck' sound when they are disturbed.

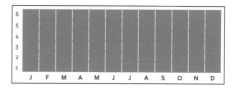

Song Thrush

The 'standard format' thrush: brown above, speckled below with a gorgeous black eye. Song Thrushes are slightly smaller than Blackbirds and, at least at Lee Abbey, a little more elusive. Song Thrushes can occasionally be seen feeding on the lawns, looking for the snails that they famously smash apart by dashing them on rocks. But they are more commonly seen (or at least heard) in the woods around the estate, where their clear, repeated song phrases carry remarkably well.

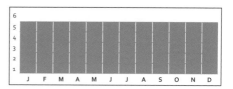

Mistle Thrush

Mistle Thrushes have a very similar plumage to Song Thrushes but they are about a third larger and carry themselves in a much more 'top-heavy' fashion. In flight, Mistle Thrushes have a small off-white bar on each wing which is, aside from the 'general feel' of the thing, the best means of separating the two species. Reasonably large flocks of Mistle Thrushes can occasionally be found in the trees around the rookery, where they are often given away by their distinctive rattling call. Their song is melodious with a slightly melancholy lilt, often delivered in all weathers, giving them their alternative country name of Stormcock.

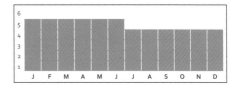

Redwing

Arriving no earlier than mid-November, fleeing their Arctic breeding grounds, Redwing are small thrushes: a deep chocolate brown on top, creamy below, with a gash of red under their wings. These are striking birds, with a stern expression. Redwings leave abruptly at the first sign of spring, usually around the beginning of March.

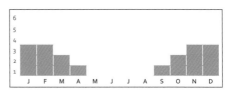

Fieldfare

Fieldfare are also winter visitors. They are larger than Redwings, with a grey and black head and slightly lighter brown body and like Redwings are often seen in flocks, which are regularly comprised of both species. Their chattering calls often give them away.

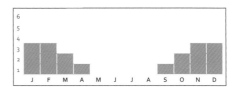

Chiffchaff

The Chiffchaff lives up to its name; its song being 'chiffchaff' repeated over and over. It is one of the earliest signs of spring, usually heard first in March. Chiffchaffs are 'leaf warblers'; small and olive green above, paler below, with a prominent 'eyebrow'. They have fine, insect eating bills and a tendency not to stay still.

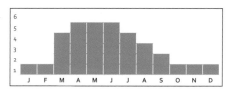

Willow Warbler

The Willow Warbler is the second most common leaf warbler to be found at Lee Abbey. Its song is much prettier than the Chiffchaff's. They sing from high up in a tree a descending, flutey melody that sounds rather like a refined chaffinch. Willow Warblers are almost identical to Chiffchaffs to look at but they have a 'cleaner', fresher plumage, with a pale cheek and pale legs (a Chiffchaff's legs are a dark brown). Their wings are, by comparison, longer than a Chiffchaff's.

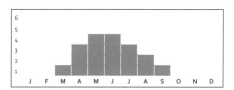

Wood Warbler

The Wood Warbler is a rare breeding bird in Britain and only breeds in Wales and small pockets of South West England. Lee Abbey's woodlands hold a few. Wood Warblers have a similar plumage to Willow Warbler's but a much greener front bib, which fades out to pure white underparts. Wood Warblers have a curious song, which is often compared to the sound of a spinning coin on a marble worktop.

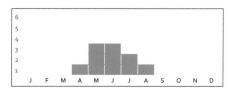

Blackcap

The Blackcap is another woodland warbler – but of a slightly different ilk. Blackcaps are larger than the leaf warblers, coming in a uniform light grey. The distinguishing feature is, of course, their inky black head – a neat beret atop the eyeline. The female's headgear is, by contrast, a rather rusty red. Blackcaps are migratory and they are reasonably gregarious with a rather beautiful song; lasting around eight seconds it begins somewhat irresolutely before falling into a melancholy, flutelike crescendo. That said, some Blackcaps do over-winter, taking advantage of the mild North Devon climate, and this can be a good time to see them - they sometimes turn up for a free meal at bird feeders

Garden Warbler

The Garden Warbler is a close relative of the Blackcap, indeed their songs are particularly hard to differentiate, though Garden Warblers tend to include longer mellow phrases in their repertoire.

Garden Warblers are scarcer than their name suggests and can be tricky to identify when seen. They can generally be distinguished by their lack of discernible features, being of an average warbler size and almost completely uniform brown from head to toe. Look out for their fine, insect eating bill, slightly dumpy body shape and small amount of grey about their 'shoulder'. They skulk around the woodland (and less frequently the gardens) between mid-April and late September.

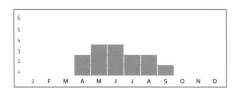

Whitethroat

The Whitethroat is another summer visitor and one that favours slightly more open, scrubby ground with thickets. In their best breeding plumage Whitethroats are smart-looking birds, with a slate-grey head, prominent white throat and rusty red lower parts. Male Whitethroats can get quite gregarious during the breeding season. They sing their scratchy warbling song often in flight; rising up from a hedge before descending again.

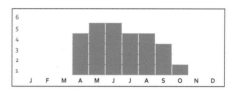

Goldcrest

Nearly a warbler but not quite, Goldcrests are the smallest birds in Britain. Messy olive green and white all over, with the exception of a remarkable golden gash running along the very top of their head. Most often heard before being seen, they have a very high-pitched whistle. Goldcrests are actually reasonably common and can be found in both deciduous and coniferous woodland. They can be incredibly hard to get good views of as they are constantly flitting around on the move, never staying still. This is fair enough, as they have to eat nearly half their weight in insects and moth eggs daily to survive winter. The best place for good views is around the yews and conifers near Jenny's.

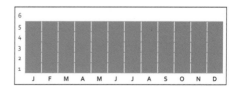

Nuthatch

A specialist of deciduous woodland, Nuthatches are one of those species that seem just as happy moving vertically on a tree as horizontally. They can regularly be seen climbing dextrously up and down tree trunks. Blue-grey above, light chestnut below, with a long, strong bill and pencil line black mascara along their eyeline. Nuthatches are robin sized, but bulky and neckless. Nuthatches can be very noisy birds. Their repertoire, which ranges from the conversational, tit-like 'twit' to more song-like phrases of 'jujujujuju', can penetrate even the densest of woodland. While the best place to see Nutchatches is generally woodland, they have been known to visit bird tables.

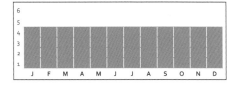

Treecreeper

Treecreepers are another vertically inclined bird. They typically fly from tree to tree, working their way up each trunk. Treecreepers are quite hard to see, so much so in fact, that it can be quite easy to mistake one for a particularly acrobatic mouse. They are small, brown above and white beneath, with a decurved bill, white 'eyebrow' and strong tail. Whilst resident, treecreepers are generally easier to see in winter, if only because there are fewer leaves in the way and a lack of food makes them marginally more gregarious.

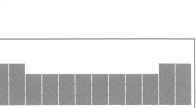

Pied Flycatcher

Another summer visitor, the Pied Flycatcher has bred in the past at Lee Abbey but is now quite rare here. The males *(above)* are smart black and white birds, slightly smaller than a robin, the females *(below)* a little drab, a mix of brown and white. Pied Flycatchers are very particular about their habitat. In Britain they only breed in western deciduous woodland, using holes to nest in with a liking for nestboxes. Their song is a rather sweet melodious ditty of a few repeated phrases.

J F M A M J J A S O N D

Spotted Flycatcher

More common and less eye-catching than their monochrome cousins, Spotted Flycatchers are nevertheless beautiful, intriguing birds in their own right. They are mottled brown, robin sized, with a small bill. Look out for their distinctive behaviour; scouting from a favoured, mid-level perch, they will repeatedly swoop to the ground to pick up insects from the floor. Spotted Flycatchers favour more open ground than Pied Flycatchers, so look for them in the copses around the Valley of Rocks between April and September. It is not really a songster; its voice can be best described as a random call of a few high-pitched notes.

J F M A M J J A S O N D

Blue Tit

Most obvious of the tit family is the ubiquitous Blue Tit, with its shocking blue forehead and wings and yellow body. In the breeding season great roving packs of newly fledged birds are shepherded to the best feeding areas (normally the gardens' feeding stations) by somewhat harried looking adults. The Blue Tit's song is a cheerful rippling tinkle, but it also has many calls, including a commonly heard scolding 'churr'.

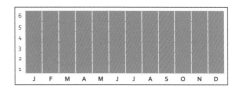

Great Tit

Great Tits are the biggest and most aggressive of the tits, with a piebald head and blue and yellow body. The males have a larger black stripe going down their front; in fact, the male with the largest stripe usually gets all the females. Listen out for their 'teacher teacher' call, especially in early spring, although it is a bird very capable of singing many variations on the theme.

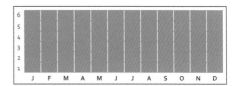

Marsh Tit

If you head into the woods you may come across Marsh Tits. They are small and drab, with black foreheads and little 'bibs'. Their call is a high-pitched sneeze ('pitch-oo'). The deciduous woodlands of North Devon are something of a haven for these mysterious birds, which are in decline in Britain.

Coal Tit

Coal tits look like miniature, washed-out Great Tits, sometimes being only half as big as them. They sometimes turn up on the feeders, but they are conifer and yew specialists, living off moth eggs and other tiny morsels. They have a, piping, 'peepee' call, so high-pitched as to be almost inaudible.

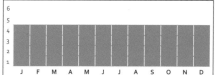

Long-tailed Tit

Long-tailed Tits are another species that works in family groups, flying through your field of vision, demanding your attention, then disappearing off into the woods. Beautiful pink black and white balls of fluff with, you guessed it, improbably long tails.

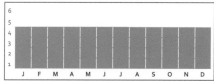

Spring is the best time to practice your bird song identification in the Lee Abbey Estate woods and glades

Chaffinch

Regular under our birdfeeders, Chaffinches can be seen anywhere in the grounds at Lee Abbey. Males have a charming song, descending from high to low, with the lilt of a farmer. It has many calls including a noticeable 'pink pink' which aptly describes the colouring of the male bird – note also the slate-grey head and bright white wing bars make them easy to spot in flight. The female is a duller buff variant of the male bird.

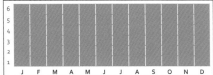

Greenfinch

Greenfinches are the bullies of the finch family. Males are a glorious green with yellow wing tips, females a little drabber like they have faded in the wash. Both have enormous, seed cracking bills and a particularly stern expression. Greenfinches are not natural singers, but they give it a good go, with their twittering song and their nasal 'zwee' calls.

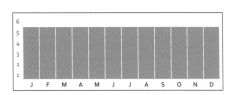

You don't have to leave the garden at Lee Abbey to have a good birdwatching experience. Many of the tit and finch species spend time between the shrubs, the large conifer trees and the bird feeders by the orangery.

Goldfinch

Goldfinches flit between the fields and gorse patches, clownishly attacking thistles. They have a bright red, blood-spattered face, framed by first white and then black. The 'gold' comes from their wing bars, which is particularly noticeable as they fly from feeding patch to feeding patch. Goldfinches are chatterers rather than singers and will constantly chatter in twinkling notes to keep track of the rest of the flock. They are regular on the bird feeders, having developed a particular liking for niger seed.

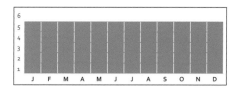

Siskin

These smart little birds are striped green, black and yellow. They are smaller than goldfinches but very similar behaviour-wise. Lee Abbey is lucky to have a few residents, whose numbers are sometimes bolstered by wintering birds fleeing the cold of their Scandinavian breeding grounds. They often announce their presence with a distinctive call-note 'tsyzing', and they are most frequently seen in small flocks.

Bullfinch

The Bullfinch is large, powerful and crimson coloured with a stocky bill and an inky black skullcap. Look out for its white rump as these shy birds fly away from you. The female is a duller purple version of the male. Its song consists of a few soft, creaky-sounding notes often uttered from deep in the undergrowth.

Linnet

Look out for roving flocks of Linnets in the farmland and, more particularly, the upland moorland areas. Small, twinkling, a flock sounds like a child with a flute. With a beautiful rosy front, russet brown body and black and white flecks, Linnets are, in their own subtle way, one of our most attractive birds. Once a staple of farmland, they are now far rarer than they used to be. Happily, Lee Abbey has a local flock of around thirty birds, which split their time almost equally between the scrubby farmland around the crosses and the Valley of Rocks.

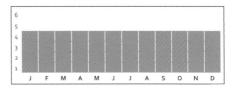

House Sparrow

House Sparrows may be another of our small brown birds, but they are easy enough to identify. Slightly stockier than Robins, males have a bold black and grey face, females a more plain affair. They have blunt, multipurpose bills, a brash, mottled chestnut back and pale grey underparts. House Sparrows are most often seen, unsurprisingly, around the houses, where there are family groups of up to 15 or so birds. House Sparrows are one of the great 'chirpers' of the bird world. They have little by way of song, but are noisy and gregarious, and will often call out a contented 'chirp'.

Starling

Starlings are another species that have seen large declines across the country – they are still, however one of our commonest birds. Song Thrush sized, with a glossy, speckled plumage that becomes a little drabber in winter. Starlings are the great entertainers of the bird world. They are great mimics; their song takes inspiration from anything from the calls of other birds to telephones. At Lee Abbey, I have heard them ripping off everything from Chaffinches to Gulls and even Buzzards.

One of the great spectacles of British wildlife is performed by starlings – their great murmurations, in which thousands of birds will dance, cavort and fly in unison before going to their winter roost. It is a spectacle that, sadly, is becoming rarer and rarer, the displays themselves smaller and smaller.

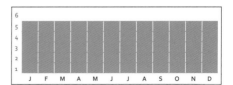

Appendix:
All birds observed during surveys 2007-2014

The following is a list of all species noted during monthly census surveys since 2007 combined with other sightings recorded on the guest notice board (2012-2014).

Fulmar
Manx Shearwater
Gannet
Cormorant
Shag
Oystercatcher
Great Black-backed Gull
Lesser Black-backed Gull
Common Gull
Black-headed Gull
Herring Gull
Kittiwake
Razorbill
Guillemot
Mallard
Red-breasted Merganser
Canada Goose
Grey Heron
Moorhen
Lapwing
Woodpigeon
Collared Dove
Stock Dove
Cuckoo
Green Woodpecker
Great Spotted Woodpecker
Skylark
Meadow Pipit
Rock Pipit
Pied Wagtail
Grey Wagtail
Yellow Wagtail
Wren
Dipper
Dunnock

Robin
Stonechat
Wheatear
Blackbird
Song Thrush
Mistle Thrush
Redwing
Fieldfare
Blackcap
Whitethroat
Willow Warbler
Wood Warbler
Garden Warbler
Grasshopper Warbler
Sedge Warbler
Chiffchaff
Goldcrest
Firecrest
Spotted Flycatcher
Pied Flycatcher
Great Tit
Blue Tit
Coal Tit
Marsh Tit
Long-tailed Tit
Nuthatch
Treecreeper
Starling
House Sparrow
Chaffinch
Linnet
Goldfinch
Siskin
Greenfinch
Bullfinch

Yellowhammer
Redstart
Dipper
Peregrine Falcon
Sparrowhawk
Kestrel
Buzzard
Red Kite
Tawny Owl
Barn Owl
Wood Pigeon
House Martin
Swallow
Swift
Magpie
Rook
Raven
Jackdaw
Jay
Pheasant